ANCIENT WARRIORS

GLADIATORS

Fly!

An Imprint of Abdo Zoom
abdobooks.com

KENNY ABDO

abdobooks.com

Published by Abdo Zoom, a division of ABDO, P.O. Box 398166, Minneapolis, Minnesota 55439. Copyright © 2021 by Abdo Consulting Group, Inc. International copyrights reserved in all countries. No part of this book may be reproduced in any form without written permission from the publisher. Fly!™ is a trademark and logo of Abdo Zoom.

Printed in the United States of America, North Mankato, Minnesota.
052020
092020

THIS BOOK CONTAINS RECYCLED MATERIALS

Photo Credits: Alamy, Everett Collection, Getty Images, iStock, newscom, North Wind Picture Archives, Shutterstock
Production Contributors: Kenny Abdo, Jennie Forsberg, Grace Hansen
Design Contributors: Dorothy Toth, Neil Klinepier, Laura Graphenteen

Library of Congress Control Number: 2019956197

Publisher's Cataloging-in-Publication Data

Names: Abdo, Kenny, author.
Title: Gladiators / by Kenny Abdo
Description: Minneapolis, Minnesota : Abdo Zoom, 2021 | Series: Ancient warriors | Includes online resources and index.
Identifiers: ISBN 9781098221225 (lib. bdg.) | ISBN 9781098222208 (ebook) | ISBN 9781098222697 (Read-to-Me ebook)
Subjects: LCSH: Gladiators--Juvenile literature. | Hand-to-hand fighting--Juvenile literature. | Rome--History--Empire, 284-476--Juvenile literature. | Soldiers-Juvenile literature.
Classification: DDC 796.8--dc23

TABLE OF CONTENTS

GLADIATORS

Entertaining the crowds of Rome's **Colosseum**, Gladiators were the superstars of warriors.

Gladiators were highly trained fighters. They fought one another to amuse audiences for more than 650 years!

THE WARRIORS

Gladiators came from many different places. Some were prisoners. Some were slaves from Africa and Europe. Others asked to fight. They were even paid.

There were also female gladiators. By the 1st century CE they had become common fighters at the games.

Portraits of fighters hung on
the walls of many public places.
Gladiators even **endorsed** products
just like athletes of today.

WARFARE & TACTICS

It is believed that the first gladiator fight was held in the 4th century BCE. The games began as celebrations of war victories.

Gladiators used swords, spears, and shields as weapons. They wore helmets and body armor for protection.

There were many different types of gladiators. Those who fought with a sword on a horse were known as equites. Thraeces were the most popular. They fought on foot with swords and shields.

Crowds started to become bored with gladiator games. So, animals like lions and bears were brought in to fight. The man versus beast shows brought new excitement to the sport.

The last gladiator battle in Rome was in 404 CE. At the game, a **monk** tried to stop a fight. He was killed and a **ban** against the events began.

19

ARE YOU NOT ENTERTAINED?!

Marcus Nonius Macrinus was the inspiration for the hit movie *Gladiator*. Russell Crowe's character, Maximus shares similar traits with Marcus, who was a Roman senator and fighter.

Being called a gladiator today means you are strong willed and physically fit. Much like the first superstar athletes in history!

GLOSSARY

ban – legally prohibited.

Colosseum – the largest stadium of the time in the center of Rome. Built in 70 CE, all major events took place there.

endorse – a celebrity or athletes' approval of a product.

monk – a member of a religious community. They live a life of poverty and obedience.

portrait – a drawing or painting of a person.

ONLINE RESOURCES

Booklinks
NONFICTION NETWORK
FREE! ONLINE NONFICTION RESOURCES

To learn more about gladiators, please visit **abdobooklinks.com** or scan this QR code. These links are routinely monitored and updated to provide the most current information available.

INDEX